Of Miracles

Of Miracles

Of Miracles

David Hume

Furnished with an Introduction and Notes by

Antony Flew

Open  Court
La Salle, Illinois

OC789   10 9 8 7 6 5 4 3 2 1

Library of Congress Cataloging in Publication Data
Hume, David, 1711–1776.
Of miracles.

(Open Court classics)
Bibliography: p.
1. Miracles—Early works to 1800. 2. Hume, David,
1711–1776—Views on miracles. I. Title.
B1499.M5H85   1985   210   85-11410
ISBN 0-912050-72-1

Introduction

by Antony Flew

1. 'Of Miracles' in Hume's work as a whole

David Hume was born in 1711 and died in 1776, the year of the American Declaration of Independence. (It was an event which he had long foreseen, and at once welcomed.) Hume's treatment 'Of Miracles' (1748) quickly became, and long remained, the most scandalous and controversial of all his works. In more recent years it has often been neglected, even by those to whom its message is most relevant. Many too of those who have studied it have, through tearing it out of context, failed fully to understand and come to terms with both its strength and its weaknesses. The purpose of the present Introduction is to provide that context, to indicate the true direction and the formidable force of Hume's argument, and to remedy those weaknesses.

Hume's first work, published anonymously before the author had turned thirty, was *A Treatise of Human Nature* (1739–40). The title is significant. For although the *Treatise* is now by common consent allowed to be one of the great classics of philosophy, by Hume himself it was seen—to employ a distinction not current in his day—not as an exotic exercise in purely professional philosophizing, but rather as a contribution to psychology and to other empirical human studies. According to the rueful retrospect of *My Own Life*, this "juvenile work . . . fell *dead-born from the press.*" Not permitting himself to be for long discouraged, Hume soon produced a second book, the two-volume *Essays, Moral and Political.*

In 1748 this was followed by the book eventually entitled *An Enquiry concerning Human Understanding.* In 1752 this first *Enquiry* was followed by a second, *An Enquiry Concerning the Principles of Morals*—as well as by the more immediately successful *Political Discourses.* In the same year, having been appointed Librarian to the Faculty of Advocates in Edinburgh, Hume started work on his *History of England.* This quickly became standard. It continued to go into fresh editions for over a century. The catalogue of the British Museum Library still lists the author as simply: "Hume, David, the historian."

The first *Enquiry* was an investigation in the genre of John Locke's *Essay concerning Human Understanding* (1690), a genre in which, later in Hume's century, both works were to be joined by the three great *Critiques* of Immanuel Kant (1724–1804). In an introductory 'Epistle to the Reader' Locke tells us how one day he and some friends, discussing unspecified grand philosophical issues, found themselves completely "at a stand" (deadlocked). It appeared that no progress would or could be achieved until and unless they first discovered what "our understanding were, or were not, fitted to deal with", what it is and is not possible for creatures such as we to find out and to know.

It is to this most fundamental investigation that both Locke's *Essay* and Hume's first *Enquiry* are devoted, while Hume's treatment 'Of Miracles' is essential to the whole project of that *Enquiry*. It was therefore originally published as Section X of *An Enquiry concerning Human Understanding*. But during the nineteenth century, in the edition of Hume's *Essays Literary Moral and Political* in Sir John Lubbock's best-selling Hundred Books series, both this Section X and the subsequent Section XI are excised, to appear only in a reluctant Appendix. This has a remarkable initial note beginning: "These essays are generally omitted in popular editions of the writings of Hume." In our own century, in what has been and is the most widely used edition of the first and second *Enquiries* together, both these sections are included in their proper places. Nevertheless the Editor in his Introduction dismisses them as an irrelevant and offensive addition, to be explained only by reference to "Hume's ambition to disturb 'the zealots' at all costs." (In *My Own Life* Hume had lamented that his *Treatise* had not achieved "such distinction as even to excite a murmer among the zealots"—by which he meant those who would be shocked by his irreligion.)

2. Hume's aim in 'Of Miracles'

This brings us to the second point which the reader of 'Of Miracles' must always hold firmly in mind. It is that Hume's prime concern here is with knowledge, and hence with evidence rather than fact. He is not asking whether any miracles have occurred or do occur—though he makes it plain that as a "wise man . . . who proportions his belief to the evidence", he is himself quite certain that they have not, and do not. Instead he is asking whether and, if so, how—even supposing that a miracle had occurred—we could know, repeat *know*, that it had. Most especially he is asking—and urging that we must answer in the negative—a more particular question: "whether a miracle can [ever] be proved, so as to be the foundation of a system of religion".

3. Miracles as evidence of true revelation

The third matter to master before starting to study 'Of Miracles' is the reason why this more particular question is both of great intrinsic importance and indispensably relevant to the whole project of this first *Enquiry*. In a nutshell, it is that there would seem to be no other way of showing that the Christian, or any rival candidate, is a genuine Revelation of the true God. To serve as the key term in such a demonstration, the word 'miracle' has to be construed (as both Hume himself and all his contemporary opponents did construe it) in a very strong sense. It must involve an overriding of a law of nature, a doing of what is known to be naturally impossible by a Power which is, by this very overriding, shown to be Supernatural and Supreme.

Only if this is given can the occurrence of a miracle under the auspices of some particular system of belief constitute an inexpugnable Divine endorsement of that system. Without appreciating the rationality and the straightforwardness of this approach to the settling of disputes between the protagonists of incompatible sets of religious beliefs, we cannot hope to understand either Hume's insistence that the miracle stories of rival religions must be assessed as not merely different but contrary, or the delighted attention which he gives to the then recent Affair of the Abbé Paris. It was precisely and only because both the Jansenists and the Jesuits did accept these principles that both parties were so keen to show, the one that miracles had occurred at that cleric's tomb, and the other that they had not.

In Section X, and in the following Section XI, Hume deploys his case against the traditional reasoned apologetic for Christianity. He tries to discredit—and, I believe, succeeds in discrediting—the whole bold attempt. Its first stage consisted in labouring to establish, by appealing only to natural reason and common experience, the existence and certain minimal characteristics of God. The second stage tried to supplement this inevitably somewhat sketchy religion of nature with a more abundant Revelation.

This programme, in its characteristically eighteenth century form, achieved archetypal fulfilment in Archdeacon William Paley's *Natural Theology* (London, 1802) and in the same author's *Evidences of Christianity* (London, 1794). Here the weight of the first part of the case was borne mainly by the Argument to Design: if from a watch we may infer a watchmaker, then surely the orderliness of the Universe entitles us to infer, by parity of reasoning, a Universe-Maker?

It is this argument which Hume attacks in Section XI, and more extensively in his posthumous masterpiece—revised finally on his deathbed—the *Dialogues concerning Natural Religion* (1779). All the other arguments are dismissed in very short order in Section XII (iii), as well as (rather less briefly) in the later work. The second part of the traditional case rested upon the claim that there is ample historical evidence to show that the Biblical miracles, including crucially the physical resurrection of Jesus bar Joseph, did in fact occur; and that this in turn proved the crucial Christian claims.

The general validity of this two-stage apologetic, although not that of any particular putative proof of Natural Theology, was defined in 1870 by the First Vatican Council as itself a dogma necessary to salvation. However, we have to notice that since the Second Vatican Council touched off the progressive Protestantization of the Roman Church this defined dogma appears to have become one item rather rarely picked by those professing Catholics who insist on choosing out of the historic deposit of the Faith their own individual anthologies of credibility. The relevant canon dealing with the second stage neither hesitates nor compromises: "If anyone shall say ... that miracles can never be known for certain, or that the divine origin of the Christian religion cannot properly be proved by them: let him be anathema."

There are many today who, while continuing to claim the Christian name, feel forced to abandon that strong conception of the miraculous, and indeed the whole rational apologetic for which it provides a crucial term. This puts them in a doubly desperate position. In the first place, they can scarcely hope to develop what too often they do not even bother to seek: any better alternative way of trying to show that their faith is reasonable. In the second place, one particular miracle story—that of what myriads of old-fashioned Easter sermons have insisted must be the miracle of miracles—is not merely evidence for the authenticity of the Christian Revelation, but is also integral to it. It is the very heart and essence of the Gospel message that the second person of the Trinity became man: that He was born of woman, if not necessarily of a virgin; that He preached the word of his Father in the Galilee; that He was crucified, dead and buried; *and that He rose again on the third day.* It was not, therefore, any wanton or gratuitous desire to shock which led Hume to introduce his factitious legend of the Resurrection of Elizabeth the Great. It was, rather, the need to press his argument home.

4. Miracles and laws of nature

That argument takes off from the observation that there cannot but be a conflict, even a contradiction, within any suitably comprehensive case for saying that a miracle has actually occurred. Such a case has to show: first, that the supposed laws, of which the actual occurrence of the putatively miraculous events would constitute an overriding, do in fact obtain; and, second, that the overridings have in fact occurred.

All evidence for the first proposition, however, is at the same time evidence against the second; and the other way about. For to say that a law of nature obtains just is to say that it is (not logically or apriori, but naturally and practically) impossible for any events to occur such that these events would by their occurring falsify the universal and nomological (law-stating) proposition which expresses that law of nature. Thus, to show that a law of nature obtains just is to show that the occurrence of exceptions is naturally impossible; while to show that even one 'exception' has occurred would be to show that that law, at least in that formulation, did not obtain.

This conflict or contradiction can be resolved; but only at what must here be an unacceptable price. Certainly it is open to spokespersons for the miraculous to claim that their alleged revelations provide them with the necessary criteria. These are the criteria which they need for distinguishing between, on the one hand, those exceptions which as overridings by a Power above and outside Nature do not constitute true falsifications of the supposed laws of nature, and on the other hand, those exceptions' which are truly falsifying—and hence call for further and hopefully more successful creative work by scientists.

It is, or ought to be, obvious why such a resolution cannot be accepted by anyone committed to the traditional apologetic. If the occurrence of a miracle is to serve as an endorsement of a candidate revelation, then we have to excogitate some means entirely independent of that putative revelation by which this guarantee itself can be recognized. A parallel objection arises if, with what has become a fasionable school in theology, you urge that miracles are not really overridings but signs. If a sign is to signify to the unbeliever, then there has to be some means independent of the doctrinal system itself whereby the signs may be identified as such, and their significations understood.

5. Two weaknesses in Hume's argument

Hume's general presentation of his argument in Part I of Section X has two serious but remediable weaknesses. The first of these arises because he has not yet altogether abandoned one hope cherished at the time of the *Treatise*. This is the hope of producing a kind of mechanics of consciousness, with principles of the association of ideas relating moments of consciousness in something like the way in which the principles of classical mechanics related the "hard, massy and impenetrable" billiard balls of atomic theory. The second is that given his distinctive account of causal necessity, and the consequent pure regularity analysis of laws of nature, Hume cannot himself provide for any substantial distinction between the extremely unusual and the authentically miraculous.

To the first of these weaknesses the best response is: to begin by appreciating what Hume was understandably, if no doubt misguidedly, trying to do; next perhaps to smile at his efforts; and finally to pass on. Take, as an example of his laughably literalistic and plonkingly quantitative interpretation of the weighing of evidence, this statement: "A hundred instances or experiments on one side, and fifty on another, afford a doubtful expectation of any event. . . . In all cases, we must balance the opposite experiments, when they are opposite, and deduct the smaller number from the greater, in order to know the exact force of the superior evidence."

The second weakness is much more serious, and much less easily remedied. Yet it is one not likely to be noticed by anyone who reads 'Of Miracles' out of context. For Hume certainly does not make explicit, and maybe he never even noticed, the upsetting implications for his present argument of earlier contentions. Thus, having considered testimony for the unusual and the marvellous, Hume continues: "But in order to increase the probability against the testimony of witnesses, let us suppose, that the fact, which they affirm, instead of being only marvellous, is really miraculous. . . ." He then proceeds to define 'a miracle' as "a violation of the laws of nature"; or, more "accurately," as "*a transgression of a law of nature by a particular volition of the Deity.*"

As a controversial move this cannot be faulted. For in this definition Hume is providing precisely and only what his chosen opponents want and need: without such a strong notion requiring the particular intervention of a Power above and greater than Nature, they could not get their act on the road at all. But Hume appears to have forgotten that he has earlier argued that there are no natural necessities and no natural impossibilities: there is only logical necessity and logical impossibility. In his view, however, even these genuine necessities and genuine impossibilities do not characterize the non-linguistic world. For all that we could know apriori, anything might be the cause of anything, while, as Hume urged in the *Treatise* but not in any later work, it is even conceivable that events might occur without any causes at all.

Among the further consequences of these radical contentions, one is that laws of nature, in so far as they are descriptive of the phenomena to which they apply, state only that ongoings of one particular sort will in fact always be accompanied by ongoings of another particular sort. They do not state, neither do they imply, that once an event of the one sort has occurred, it must be impossible by any human or other natural force to prevent the occurrence of an event of the other sort. Laws of nature, therefore, as thus understood—or rather misunderstood—by Hume could provide no purchase for any overriding manifestations of the definitionally Supernatural Deity.

Again, Humean causes are only followed by, they do not bring about, their effects: the occurrence of the cause event, that is, does not either make necessary the occurrence of the effect event or make impossible its non-occurrence. The only necessity involved, according to Hume, is a muddled notion in us as we think about causes. It is a matter of our feeling the force of habitual associations of corresponding ideas, and projecting this muddle out onto realities among which there are to be found no necessities of any kind.

It is not possible here to essay a comprehensive and constructive critique of Hume's accounts of causation and of laws of nature. Sufficient indeed for the moment to have brought out their relevant consequences, and in that way to have suggested that for us the most promising course is to proceed as if we had never heard of Hume's denials of natural necessity and natural impossibility. That, after all, is how in our present context Hume himself proceeded!

6. Evaluating historical evidence

So far we have followed Hume in concentrating upon the question of proving a miracle "so as to be the foundation of a system of religion." But the argument expounded in Part I has a far more extensive application. It is, he claims there, "a decisive argument . . . which must at least silence the most arrogant bigotry and superstition, and free us from their impertinent solicitations . . . an argument which . . . will . . . with the wise and learned, be an everlasting check to all kinds of superstitious delusion. . . ."

It is sometimes thought that there is no more to this "everlasting check" than a trite reminder that, because the occurrence of a miracle must be very improbable, it needs to be quite exceptionally well evidenced. But C. S. Peirce, who seems never to have exploited it fully, had the vital clue in his hands when he remarked: "The whole of modern 'higher criticism' of ancient history in general . . . is based upon the same logic as is used by Hume." The truth is that this section of 'Of Miracles' belongs not only to the philosophy of religion but also to the philosophy of history. It has too a major bearing on the philosophy of science in general, and, in particular, on that of the would-be science of parapsychology.

What, with some lapses and hesitations, Hume is contending is that the criteria by which we must assess historical testimony, and the general presumptions which alone allow us to interpret the detritus of the past as historical evidence, must inevitably rule out any possibility of establishing definitively, upon purely historical evidence, that some genuinely miraculous event has occurred.

His fundamental theses are: first, that the detritus of the past cannot be construed as any sort of historical evidence unless we presume that the same basic regularities obtained then as obtain today; and second, that in trying as best he may to determine what actually happened, the historian has to employ as criteria all his present knowledge and presumed knowledge of what is probable or improbable, possible or impossible. In his *Treatise* (II [iii] 1), Hume had argued that it is only upon such presumptions that we can justify even the basic conclusion that certain kinds of ink marks on old pieces of paper constitute testimonial evidence. Earlier in his first *Enquiry* (VIII [i]), he had urged the inescapable importance of having such criteria; while, in what was originally a footnote to 'Of Miracles', he quotes with approval the reasoning of the famous physician De Sylva in the contested case of a Mademoiselle Thibaut. "It was impossible she could have been so ill as was proved by witnesses, because it was impossible that she could, in so short a time, have recovered so perfectly as he found her."

Two serious faults in Hume's presentation may obscure the force and soundness of De Sylva's reasoning and the fact that this sort of application of canons to evidence is absolutely essential to the very possibility of critical history. The first is that, contrary to his own sceptical principles, Hume tends to take it for granted that what in his own day he and all his fellow persons of sense firmly believed about the order of nature constituted not just well-grounded, yet always humanly fallible opinion, but the definitive and incorrigible last word. He is thus betrayed into rejecting as downright impossible certain reported phenomena which the progress of abnormal psychology and psychosomatic medicine has since shown to have been perfectly possible.

For instance: like other eighteenth century sceptics Hume makes much of the miracles supposedly wrought in Egypt by the soldier Emperor Vespasian, suggesting, if never outright stating, that the evidence in this case is far and away stronger than that for any of the miracle stories of the *New Testament.* Suppose that we are so conscientiously curious as to refer to the accounts given in the Roman historians Suetonius and Tacitus. We find that, according to Suetonius, when the Emperor was in Egypt "two labourers, one blind and the other lame, approached him, begging to be healed; apparently the god Serapis had promised them in a dream that if Vespasian would consent to spit in the blind man's eye and touch the lame man's leg with his heel, both would be cured." According to the longer account in Tacitus (in which the lame man becomes a man with a withered hand), Vespasian "asked the

doctors for an opinion whether blindness and
atrophy of this sort were curable by human means.
The doctors were eloquent about the various
possibilities: the blind man's vision was not
completely destroyed, and, if certain impediments
were removed, his sight would return; the other
man's limb had been dislocated, but could be put
right by correct treatment. . . . Anyway, if a cure
were effected, the credit would go to the ruler; if it
failed, the poor wretches would have to bear the
ridicule." Both historians go on to tell us that
Vespasian did what he had been asked to do,
and that the two patients were in consequence
cured.

So, given those medical reports insisting on the
absence of any gross organic lesions, and in the
light of what has since been learned about
psychosomatic possibilities, we now have to say:
not that Vespasian did after all perform two
miracles of healing during his Egyptian tour, and
that this is something which we now know on
sound historical grounds; but that what Hume
dismissed as something which could not have
occurred, because its occurrence would have been
miraculous, in fact did occur, but was not
miraculous. Our reason for saying that the cures
were indeed effected is at the same time our reason
for saying that they were not miraculous.

Before moving on to the second fault in Hume's
presentation let us notice another case equally
Classical but much less disputed. In Herodotus,
"the father of critical history", we read that at the
time of the Pharaoh Necho II (about 600 B.C.)
Phoenician sailors claimed to have circumnavigated
Africa. They said that they had sailed South down

what we call the Red Sea and arrived at the
Mediterranean coast of Egypt nearly three years
later. The interesting thing for us is their report
that during the voyage the position of the sun
shifted from the South to the North, and back
again. Herodotus, recording that they said this,
states that he himself does not believe what they
said. He had two good reasons for disbelief: first,
he knew that Phoenician and other sailors were apt
to tell tall tales; and second, he took it that he
knew that what the sailors reported was
impossible. Herodotus therefore had good reason to
dismiss this story, and did dismiss it.

But for us, what was for Herodotus an excellent
reason for incredulity is the decisive ground for
believing that Phoenicians did in fact
circumnavigate Africa at this time. They could
scarcely have got this thing about the changing
relative position of the Sun right unless they had
actually made the voyage which they said they had
made. Both Herodotus and the successors who have
on this point put him right were employing the
same sound historical methods, the only methods
possible for the critical historian.

Both he and we, that is, are and cannot but be
committed, in interpreting and assessing the
detritus of the past as historical evidence, to
appealing to all that we know or think we know
about what is probable or improbable, possible or
impossible. Thus Herodotus, in trying to interpret
the evidence of the Phoenicians, rightly appealed to
what he knew, or thought he knew, about
astronomy and geography. We, following exactly
the same fundamental principles of historical
reconstruction, but having the advantage over him

of knowing more about astronomy and geography, reach different conclusions, albeit by fundamentally the same methods.

The second serious fault in Hume's presentation arises from the inadequacies of his accounts of causation and of laws of nature, inadequacies briefly indicated in Section 4 above. This second fault is that Hume is unable to make clear why, if we are confronted with what appears to be overwhelmingly strong evidence for some occurrence believed to be impossible, it must almost if not quite always be wrong to conclude that that event did after all occur rather than that we have been mistaken in believing it impossible. Hume does concede that circumstances could arise in which we ought to admit the occurrence, and therefore reject the proposition which previously we had believed to express a law of nature. But the rationale supplied is quite inadequate.

Suppose, Hume writes, that "all authors in all languages, agree that from the first of January, 1600, there was a total darkness over the whole earth for eight days; suppose that the tradition of this extraordinary event is still strong and lively among the people; that all travellers who return from foreign countries bring us accounts of the same tradition without the least variation or contradiction—it is evident that our present philosophers, instead of doubting the fact, ought to receive it as certain and ought to search for the causes whence it might be derived."

A more manageably plausible example can be produced by supposing that European astronomers, when word first reached them of the eclipse observations made centuries earlier in China, had been committed to a theory precluding the occurrence of any eclipses visible at any of the times or in any of the places listed in the Chinese records. Then, if there was no independent reason for suspecting the truth of those Chinese observations—no state ideology, for instance, to be supported by the occurrence of eclipses in those places and at those times—it would surely have been right for the European astronomers, after admitting that they seemed to have been on the wrong track, to get back to their theoretical drawing boards. Our past philosophers, as Hume might have put it, instead of doubting the Chinese facts, ought to have received them as certain, and ought to have searched for the causes whence they might have been derived.

The crux here is again a matter of actual and possible evidence. The historical propositions, the propositions stating that an eclipse was visible in such and such a place at such and such a time, are all singular and in the past tense. It is always and necessarily too late now for any direct verification or falsification. If we are ever to discover what actually happened, this can only be by finding something present which can be interpreted as evidence, and by assessing what and how much that available evidence shows.

It is altogether different with nomological propositions; propositions, that is, which state that causal connections or laws of nature obtain; and which necessarily imply something about practical necessity and practical impossibility. Nomological propositions are open and general and can, at least in principle, be tested for truth or falsity at any time or in any place. Precisely that is why it is reasonable and right for the critical historian to employ all available confirmed nomologicals as canons of exclusion, ruling out many conceivable and even sometimes seemingly well-evidenced occurrences as practically impossible. Yet in doing this our historians should always be aware that steady advances in our knowledge of nomologicals, and occasional upsets revealing that what we had believed to constitute such knowledge was not, may demand historical reassessments—as in the cases of the supposed miracles of Vespasian and the alleged Phoenician circumnavigation of Africa.

7. Miracles of parapsychology

At the very beginning of 'Of Miracles' Hume, as we have seen, expresses the confident hope that he is about to offer "an argument which . . . will . . . with the wise and learned, be an everlasting check to all kinds of superstitious delusion. . . ." Certainly he would have rated the claims of parapsychology among those "impertinent solicitations" from which he was promising to free us. Nor is there any doubt but that his argument is relevant. For parapsychology is the would-be science of the paranormal, while that in turn is implicitly defined in terms of incompatibility with various normal beliefs about the practically impossible.

These putative phenomena are best labelled, in a studiously theory-neutral way, the psi-phenomena. This genus is then divided into two species: psi-gamma; and psi-kappa. The former includes all varieties of what used to be called Extrasensory Perception (ESP): telepathy, that is to say, and clairvoyance, whether retrocognitive, simultaneous, or precognitive. The latter is, in effect, a more non-committal word for psychokinesis (etymologically, 'movement by the mind').

It is usual to maintain that the phenomena, or alleged phenomena, of parapsychology are, or would be, non-physical or even outright incompatible with physics. But what such psi-phenomena are or would be incompatible with is not, or not primarily, any particular named law of physics: Boyle's Law, or what have you. Instead they do or would—as Hume liked to say—violate something far more universal and fundamental. What rules them out as impossible are some of what have been identified as our "basic limiting principles"; principles which together constitute a framework for all our everyday thinking about, and investigation of, human affairs; and principles which are continually being verified by our discoveries.

If, for instance, official secret information gets out from a government office, then the security people try to think of every possible channel of leakage; and what never appears on the check lists of such practical persons is psi-gamma. When similarly there has been an explosion in a power station or other industrial plant, then the investigators move in. At no stage will they entertain any suggestion that no one and nothing touched anything, that the explosion was triggered by some conscious or unconscious exercise of psi-kappa. Nor shall we expect them to turn up any reason for thinking that their, and our, framework assumptions were here mistaken.

It is, therefore, not surprising that sceptics should have redeployed Hume's argument as a challenge to the parapsychologists. In 1955, for instance, *Science* published a paper by G. R. Price doing precisely that (Vol. CXXII, No. 3165, pp. 359–367). This brought a strong response from Paul Meehl and Michael Scriven: "Price is in exactly the position of a man who might have insisted that Michelson and Morley were liars because the evidence for the physical theory of that time was stronger than that for the veracity of the experimenters."

It is most important to appreciate the reasons why this is not so. The first reason is that the Michelson-Morley experiment was *not* one member of a long series including many impressively disillusioning examples of fraud and self-deception. By contrast the history of parapsychology is full both of supposedly decisive demonstrations and of investigators of allegedly impeccable integrity, which and who have later been exposed as fraudulent. Testimony in this area would appear to suffer all the corruptions believed by Hume to afflict the foundations of "systems of religion". For the issues are, in a more modern terminology, ideologically sensitive.

Second, there was in the Michelson-Morley case no reason at the time—nor has any such reason emerged since—to suspect that the experiment would not be repeatable, and repeated; as well as confirmed indirectly by other experiments similarly repeatable and repeated. But in parapsychology there are no regularly and reliably repeatable experiments; indeed there is no regularly and reliably repeatable demonstration of the reality of any psi-phenomenon. (This is, incidentally, the reason why the Parapsychological Association ought never to have been permitted to affiliate to the American Association for the Advancement of Science, and should be expelled forthwith; unless affiliation is intended to be a tribute to scientific intentions rather than scientific achievement.)

Third, there is no even halfway plausible theory to account for the occurrence of psi-phenomena. This deficiency bears on the question of scientific status in two ways. For a theory which related the putative psi-phenomena to something else less contentious would tend both to probabilify their actual occurrence and to explain why they do thus indeed occur. Here we have the third reason why to refuse to accept the reality of such phenomena is not on all fours with dismissing the result of the Michelson-Morley experiment. For, even if no one then was ready immediately with an alternative theory, still in that case there was no good reason to fear that such a theory could not be produced. But, in the case of parapsychology now, our investigators have had a hundred years for theoretical cogitation; from which labours they have as yet brought forth nothing.

These three objections reinforce one another. So, until and unless someone comes up with a reliably and regularly repeatable demonstration of some psi-phenomenon, we shall continue to have no sufficient reason to abandon any of those basic limiting principles which support the conclusions that all such phenomena are in fact impossible. The most generous verdict which can be brought in

by a jury of wise men, who, as good Humeans
proportion their belief to the evidence—and
would not even this verdict be too generous?—is
a damping, and appropriately Scottish, 'Not
proven!'

PREFATORY NOTE

The text is exactly as Hume wrote it, except for the
following modifications.

Three of Hume's footnotes to 'Of Miracles' are so
substantial and readable that I have incorporated them into
the main body of the text. In each case where this has been
done, it is indicated in my own notes at the back. All the
contents of Hume's notes are included in either the text or my
notes.

A few spellings have been modernized. I have changed
'cotemporary' to 'contemporary', 'Arragon' to 'Aragon',
'substract' to 'subtract', and 'encrease' to 'increase'.

Antony Flew

Part 1.

There is, in Dr. Tillotson's writings, an argument against the *real presence*, which is as concise, and elegant, and strong as any argument can possibly be supposed against a doctrine, so little worthy of a serious refutation.[1] It is acknowledged on all hands, says that learned prelate, that the authority, either of the scripture or of tradition, is founded merely in the testimony of the apostles, who were eye-witnesses to those miracles of our Saviour, by which he proved his divine mission. Our evidence, then, for the truth of the *Christian* religion is less than the evidence for the truth of our senses; because, even in the first authors of our religion, it was no greater; and it is evident it must diminish in passing from them to their disciples; nor can any one rest such confidence in their testimony, as in the immediate object of his senses. But a weaker evidence can never destroy a stronger; and therefore, were the doctrine of the real presence ever so clearly revealed in scripture, it were directly contrary to the rules of just reasoning to give our assent to it. It contradicts sense, though both the scripture and tradition, on which it is supposed to be built, carry not such evidence with them as sense; when they are considered merely as external evidences, and are not brought home to every one's breast, by the immediate operation of the Holy Spirit.

Nothing is so convenient as a decisive argument of this kind, which must at least *silence* the most arrogant bigotry and superstition, and free us from their impertinent solicitations. I flatter myself, that I have discovered an argument of a like nature which, if just, will, with the wise and learned, be an everlasting check to all kinds of superstitious delusion, and, consequently, will be useful as long as the world endures; for so long, I presume, will the accounts of miracles and prodigies be found in all history, sacred and profane.

Though experience be our only guide in reasoning concerning matters of fact, it must be acknowledged that this guide is not altogether infallible, but in some cases is apt to lead us into errors. One who in our climate should expect better weather in any week of June than in one of December would reason justly and conformably to experience; but it is certain that he may happen, in the event, to find himself mistaken. However, we may observe that in such a case he would have no cause to complain of experience; because it commonly informs us beforehand of the uncertainty, by that contrariety of events which we may learn from a diligent observation. All effects follow not with like certainty from their supposed causes. Some events are found, in all countries and all ages, to have been constantly conjoined together; others are found to have been more variable, and sometimes to disappoint our expectations, so that in our reasonings concerning matter of fact there are all imaginable degrees of assurance, from the highest certainty to the lowest species of moral evidence.[2]

A wise man, therefore, proportions his belief to the evidence. In such conclusions as are founded on an infallible experience, he expects the event with the last degree of assurance, and regards his past experience as a full *proof* of the future existence of that event. In other cases, he proceeds with more caution: He weighs the opposite experiments:[3] He considers which side is supported by the greater number of experiments: to that side he inclines, with doubt and hesitation; and when at last he fixes his judgement, the evidence exceeds not what we properly call *probability*. All probability, then, supposes an opposition of experiments and observations, where the one side is found to overbalance the other, and to produce a degree of evidence, proportioned to the superiority. A hundred instances or experiments on one side, and fifty on another, afford a doubtful expectation of any event; though a hundred uniform experiments, with only one that is contradictory, reasonably beget a pretty strong degree of assurance. In all cases, we must balance the opposite experiments, where they are opposite, and deduct the smaller number from the greater, in order to know the exact force of the superior evidence.

To apply these principles to a particular instance; we may observe, that there is no species of reasoning more common, more useful, and even necessary to human life, than that which is derived from the testimony of men, and the reports of eye-witnesses and spectators. This species of reasoning, perhaps, one may deny to be founded on the relation of cause and effect. I shall not dispute about a word. It will be sufficient to observe that our assurance in any argument of this kind is derived from no other principle than our observation of the veracity of human testimony, and of the usual conformity of facts to the reports of witnesses. It being a general maxim, that no objects have any discoverable connexion together, and that all the inferences, which we can draw from one to another, are founded merely on our experience of their constant and regular conjunction; it is evident, that we ought not to make an exception to this maxim in favour of human testimony, whose connexion with any event seems, in itself, as little necessary as any other. Were not the memory tenacious to a certain degree; had not men commonly an inclination to truth and a principle of probity; were they not sensible to shame, when detected in a falsehood: Were not these, I say, discovered by *experience* to be qualities, inherent in human nature, we should never repose the least confidence in human testimony. A man delirious, or noted for falsehood and villany, has no manner of authority with us.

And as the evidence, derived from witnesses and human testimony, is founded on past experience, so it varies with the experience, and is regarded either as a *proof* or a *probability*, according as the conjunction between any particular kind of report and any kind of object has been found to be constant or variable. There are a number of circumstances to be taken into consideration in all judgements of this kind; and the ultimate standard, by which we determine all disputes, that may arise concerning them, is always derived from experience and observation. Where this experience is not entirely uniform on any side, it is attended with an unavoidable contrariety in our judgements, and with the same opposition and mutual destruction of argument as in every other kind of evidence. We frequently hesitate concerning the reports of others. We balance the opposite circumstances, which cause any doubt or uncertainty; and when we discover a superiority on any side, we incline to it; but still with a diminution of assurance, in proportion to the force of its antagonist.

This contrariety of evidence, in the present case, may be derived from several different causes; from the opposition of contrary testimony; from the character or number of the witnesses; from the manner of their delivering their testimony; or from the union of all these circumstances. We entertain a suspicion concerning any matter of fact, when the witnesses contradict each other; when they are but few, or of a doubtful character; when they have an interest in what they affirm; when they deliver their testimony with hesitation, or on the contrary, with too violent asseverations. There are many other particulars of the same kind, which may diminish or destroy the force of any argument, derived from human testimony.

Suppose, for instance, that the fact, which the testimony endeavours to establish, partakes of the extraordinary and the marvellous; in that case, the evidence, resulting from the testimony, admits of a diminution, greater or less, in proportion as the fact is more or less unusual. The reason why we place any credit in witnesses and historians, is not derived from any *connexion*, which we perceive *a priori*, between testimony and reality, but because we are accustomed to find a conformity between them. But when the fact attested is such a one as has seldom fallen under our observation, here is a contest of two opposite experiences; of which the one destroys the other, as far as its force goes, and the superior can only operate on the mind by the force, which remains. The very same principle of experience, which gives us a certain degree of assurance in the testimony of witnesses, gives us also, in this case, another degree of assurance against the fact, which they endeavour to establish; from which contradiction there necessarily arises a counterpoize, and mutual destruction of belief and authority.

I should not believe such a story were it told me by Cato, was a proverbial saying in Rome, even during the lifetime of that philosophical patriot.[4] The incredibility of a fact, it was allowed, might invalidate so great an authority.

The Indian prince, who refused to believe the first relations concerning the effects of frost, reasoned justly; and it naturally required very strong testimony to engage his assent to facts, that arose from a state of nature, with which he was unacquainted, and which bore so little analogy to those events, of which he had had constant and uniform experience. Though they were not contrary to his experience, they were not conformable to it.[5]

No Indian, it is evident, could have experience that water did not freeze in cold climates. This is placing nature in a situation quite unknown to him; and it is impossible for him to tell *a priori* what will result from it. It is making a new experiment, the consequence of which is always uncertain. One may sometimes conjecture from analogy what will follow; but still this is but conjecture. And it must be confessed that, in the present case of freezing, the event follows contrary to the rules of analogy, and is such as a rational Indian would not look for. The operations of cold upon water are not gradual, according to the degrees of cold; but whenever it comes to the freezing point, the water passes in a moment from the utmost liquidity to perfect hardness.

Such an event, therefore, may be denominated *extraordinary*, and requires a pretty strong testimony, to render it credible to people in a warm climate: But still it is not *miraculous*, nor contrary to uniform experience of the course of nature in cases where all the circumstances are the same. The inhabitants of Sumatra have always seen water fluid in their own climate, and the freezing of their rivers ought to be deemed a prodigy: But they never saw water in Muscovy during the winter; and therefore they cannot reasonably be positive what would there be the consequence.[6]

But in order to increase the probability against the testimony of witnesses, let us suppose, that the fact, which they affirm, instead of being only marvellous, is really miraculous; and suppose also, that the testimony considered apart and in itself, amounts to an entire proof; in that case, there is proof against proof, of which the strongest must prevail, but still with a diminution of its force, in proportion to that of its antagonist.

A miracle is a violation of the laws of nature; and as a firm and unalterable experience has established these laws, the proof against a miracle, from the very nature of the fact, is as entire as any argument from experience can possibly be imagined. Why is it more than probable, that all men must die; that lead cannot, of itself, remain suspended in the air; that fire consumes wood, and is extinguished by water; unless it be, that these events are found agreeable to the laws of nature, and there is required a violation of these laws, or in other words, a miracle to prevent them? Nothing is esteemed a miracle, if it ever happen in the common course of nature. It is no miracle that a man, seemingly in good health, should die on a sudden: because such a kind of death, though more unusual than any other, has yet been frequently observed to happen. But it is a miracle, that a dead man should come to life; because that has never been observed in any age or country. There must, therefore, be a uniform experience against every miraculous event, otherwise the event would not merit that appellation. And as a uniform experience amounts to a proof, there is here a direct and full *proof*, from the nature of the fact, against the existence of any miracle; nor can such a proof be destroyed, or the miracle rendered credible, but by an opposite proof, which is superior.

Sometimes an event may not, *in itself, seem* to be contrary to the laws of nature, and yet, if it were real, it might, by reason of some circumstances, be denominated a miracle; because, in *fact*, it is contrary to these laws. Thus if a person claiming a divine authority should command a sick person to be well, a healthful man to fall down dead, the clouds to pour rain, the winds to blow—in short, should order many natural events, which immediately follow upon his command—these might justly be esteemed miracles, because they are really, in this case, contrary to the laws of nature. For if any suspicion remain that the event and command concurred by accident, there is no miracle and no transgression of the laws of nature. If this suspicion be removed, there is evidently a miracle, and a transgression of these laws; because nothing can be more contrary to nature than that the voice or command of a man should have such an influence. A miracle may be accurately defined, *a transgression of a law of nature by a particular volition of the Deity, or by the interposition of some invisible agent.* A miracle may either be discovered by men or not. This alters not its nature and essence. The raising of a house or ship into the air is a visible miracle. The raising of a feather, when the wind wants ever so little of a force requisite for that purpose, is as real a miracle, though not so sensible with regard to us.[7]

The plain consequence is (and it is a general maxim worthy of our attention), 'That no testimony is sufficient to establish a miracle, unless the testimony be of such a kind, that its falsehood would be more miraculous, than the fact, which it endeavours to establish; and even in that case there is a mutual destruction of arguments, and the superior only gives us an assurance suitable to that degree of force, which remains, after deducting the inferior.' When anyone tells me, that he saw a dead man restored to life, I immediately consider with myself, whether it be more probable, that this person should either deceive or be deceived, or that the fact, which he relates, should really have happened. I weigh the one miracle against the other; and according to the superiority, which I discover, I pronounce my decision, and always reject the greater miracle. If the falsehood of his testimony would be more miraculous, than the event which he relates; then, and not till then, can he pretend to command my belief or opinion.

Part 2.

In the foregoing reasoning we have supposed, that the testimony, upon which a miracle is founded, may possibly amount to an entire proof, and that the falsehood of that testimony would be a real prodigy: But it is easy to shew, that we have been a great deal too liberal in our concession, and that there never was a miraculous event established on so full an evidence.

For *first*, there is not to be found, in all history, any miracle attested by a sufficient number of men, of such unquestioned good-sense, education, and learning, as to secure us against all delusion in themselves; of such undoubted integrity, as to place them beyond all suspicion of any design to deceive others; of such credit and reputation in the eyes of mankind, as to have a great deal to lose in case of their being detected in any falsehood; and at the same time, attesting facts performed in such a public manner and in so celebrated a part of the world, as to render the detection unavoidable: All

which circumstances are requisite to give us a full
assurance in the testimony of men.

Secondly. We may observe in human nature a
principle which, if strictly examined, will be found
to diminish extremely the assurance, which we
might, from human testimony, have, in any kind of
prodigy. The maxim, by which we commonly
conduct ourselves in our reasonings, is, that the
objects, of which we have no experience, resemble
those, of which we have; that what we have found
to be most usual is always most probable; and that
where there is an opposition of arguments, we
ought to give the preference to such as are founded
on the greatest number of past observations. But
though, in proceeding by this rule, we readily reject
any fact which is unusual and incredible in an
ordinary degree; yet in advancing farther, the mind
observes not always the same rule; but when
anything is affirmed utterly absurd and miraculous,
it rather the more readily admits of such a fact,
upon account of that very circumstance, which
ought to destroy all its authority. The passion of
surprise and *wonder*, arising from miracles, being
an agreeable emotion, gives a sensible tendency
towards the belief of those events, from which it is
derived. And this goes so far, that even those who
cannot enjoy this pleasure immediately, nor can
believe those miraculous events, of which they are
informed, yet love to partake of the satisfaction at
second-hand or by rebound, and place a pride and
delight in exciting the admiration of others.

With what greediness are the miraculous
accounts of travellers received, their descriptions of
sea and land monsters, their relations of wonderful
adventures, strange men, and uncouth manners?

But if the spirit of religion join itself to the love of wonder, there is an end of common sense; and human testimony, in these circumstances, loses all pretensions to authority. A religionist may be an enthusiast,[8] and imagine he sees what has no reality: he may know his narrative to be false, and yet persevere in it, with the best intentions in the world, for the sake of promoting so holy a cause: or even where this delusion has not place, vanity, excited by so strong a temptation, operates on him more powerfully than on the rest of mankind in any other circumstances; and self-interest with equal force. His auditors may not have, and commonly have not, sufficient judgement to canvass his evidence: what judgement they have, they renounce by principle, in these sublime and mysterious subjects: or if they were ever so willing to employ it, passion and a heated imagination disturb the regularity of its operations. Their credulity increases his impudence: and his impudence overpowers their credulity.

Eloquence, when at its highest pitch, leaves little room for reason or reflection; but addressing itself entirely to the fancy or the affections, captivates the willing hearers, and subdues their understanding. Happily, this pitch it seldom attains. But what a Tully or a Demosthenes could scarcely effect over a Roman or Athenian audience, every *Capuchin*, every itinerant or stationary teacher can perform over the generality of mankind, and in a higher degree, by touching such gross and vulgar passions.[9]

The many instances of forged miracles, and prophecies, and supernatural events, which, in all ages, have either been detected by contrary evidence, or which detect themselves by their absurdity, prove sufficiently the strong propensity of mankind to the extraordinary and the marvellous, and ought reasonably to beget a suspicion against all relations of this kind. This is our natural way of thinking, even with regard to the most common and most credible events. For instance: There is no kind of report which rises so easily, and spreads so quickly, especially in country places and provincial towns, as those concerning marriages; insomuch that two young persons of equal condition never see each other twice, but the whole neighbourhood immediately join them together. The pleasure of telling a piece of news so interesting, of propagating it, and of being the first reporters of it, spreads the intelligence. And this is so well known, that no man of sense gives attention to these reports, till he find them confirmed by some greater evidence. Do not the same passions, and others still stronger, incline the generality of mankind to believe and report, with the greatest vehemence and assurance, all religious miracles?

Thirdly. It forms a strong presumption against all supernatural and miraculous relations, that they are observed chiefly to abound among ignorant and barbarous nations; or if a civilized people has ever given admission to any of them, that people will be found to have received them from ignorant and barbarous ancestors, who transmitted them with that inviolable sanction and authority, which always attend received opinions. When we peruse the first histories of all nations, we are apt to imagine ourselves transported into some new world; where the whole frame of nature is disjointed, and every element performs its operations in a different manner, from what it does at present. Battles, revolutions, pestilence, famine and death, are never the effect of those natural causes, which we experience. Prodigies, omens, oracles, judgements, quite obscure the few natural events, that are intermingled with them. But as the former grow thinner every page, in proportion as we advance nearer the enlightened ages, we soon learn, that there is nothing mysterious or supernatural in the case, but that all proceeds from the usual propensity of mankind towards the marvellous, and that, though this inclination may at intervals receive a check from sense and learning, it can never be thoroughly extirpated from human nature.

It is strange, a judicious reader is apt to say, upon the perusal of these wonderful historians, *that such prodigious events never happen in our days*. But it is nothing strange, I hope, that men should lie in all ages. You must surely have seen instances enough of that frailty. You have yourself heard many such marvellous relations started, which, being treated with scorn by all the wise and judicious, have at last been abandoned even by the vulgar. Be assured, that those renowned lies, which have spread and flourished to such a monstrous height, arose from like beginnings; but being sown in a more proper soil, shot up at last into prodigies almost equal to those which they relate.

It was a wise policy in that false prophet, Alexander, who though now forgotten, was once so famous, to lay the first scene of his impostures in Paphlagonia, where, as Lucian tells us, the people were extremely ignorant and stupid, and ready to swallow even the grossest delusion.[10] People at a

distance, who are weak enough to think the matter
at all worth enquiry, have no opportunity of
receiving better information. The stories come
magnified to them by a hundred circumstances.
Fools are industrious in propagating the imposture;
while the wise and learned are contented, in
general, to deride its absurdity, without informing
themselves of the particular facts, by which it may
be distinctly refuted. And thus the impostor above
mentioned was enabled to proceed, from his
ignorant Paphlagonians, to the enlisting of votaries,
even among the Grecian philosophers, and men of
the most eminent rank and distinction in Rome:
nay, could engage the attention of that sage
emperor Marcus Aurelius,[11] so far as to make him
trust the success of a military expedition to his
delusive prophecies.

The advantages are so great, of starting an
imposture among an ignorant people, that, even
though the delusion should be too gross to impose
on the generality of them *(which, though seldom, is
sometimes the case)* it has a much better chance for
succeeding in remote countries, than if the first
scene had been laid in a city renowned for arts and
knowledge. The most ignorant and barbarous of
these barbarians carry the report abroad. None of
their countrymen have a large correspondence, or
sufficient credit and authority to contradict and
beat down the delusion. Men's inclination to the
marvellous has full opportunity to display itself.
And thus a story, which is universally exploded in
the place where it was first started, shall pass for
certain at a thousand miles distance. But had
Alexander fixed his residence at Athens, the
philosophers of that renowned mart of learning had

immediately spread, throughout the whole Roman
empire, their sense of the matter; which, being
supported by so great authority, and displayed by
all the force of reason and eloquence, had entirely
opened the eyes of mankind. It is true; Lucian,
passing by chance through Paphlagonia, had an
opportunity of performing this good office. But,
though much to be wished, it does not always
happen, that every Alexander meets with a Lucian,
ready to expose and detect his impostures.

I may add as a *fourth* reason, which diminishes
the authority of prodigies, that there is no
testimony for any, even those which have not been
expressly detected, that is not opposed by an
infinite number of witnesses; so that not only the
miracle destroys the credit of testimony, but the
testimony destroys itself. To make this the better
understood, let us consider, that, in matters of
religion, whatever is different is contrary; and that
it is impossible the religions of ancient Rome, of
Turkey, of Siam, and of China should, all of them,
be established on any solid foundation. Every
miracle, therefore, pretended to have been wrought
in any of these religions (and all of them abound in
miracles), as its direct scope is to establish the
particular system to which it is attributed; so has it
the same force, though more indirectly, to
overthrow every other system. In destroying a rival
system, it likewise destroys the credit of those
miracles, on which that system was established; so
that all the prodigies of different religions are to be
regarded as contrary facts, and the evidences of
these prodigies, whether weak or strong, as
opposite to each other. According to this method of
reasoning, when we believe any miracle of

Mahomet or his successors,[12] we have for our warrant the testimony of a few barbarous Arabians: And on the other hand, we are to regard the authority of Titus Livius, Plutarch, Tacitus, and, in short, of all the authors and witnesses, Grecian, Chinese, and Roman Catholic, who have related any miracle in their particular religion;[13] I say, we are to regard their testimony in the same light as if they had mentioned that Mahometan miracle, and had in express terms contradicted it, with the same certainty as they have for the miracle they relate. This argument may appear over subtile and refined; but is not in reality different from the reasoning of a judge, who supposes, that the credit of two witnesses, maintaining a crime against any one, is destroyed by the testimony of two others, who affirm him to have been two hundred leagues distant, at the same instant when the crime is said to have been committed.

One of the best attested miracles in all profane history, is that which Tacitus reports of Vespasian,[14] who cured a blind man in Alexandria, by means of his spittle, and a lame man by the mere touch of his foot; in obedience to a vision of the god Serapis, who had enjoined them to have recourse to the Emperor, for these miraculous cures. The story may be seen in that fine historian;[15] where every circumstance seems to add weight to the testimony, and might be displayed at large with all the force of argument and eloquence, if any one were now concerned to enforce the evidence of that exploded and idolatrous superstition. The gravity, solidity, age, and probity of so great an emperor, who, through the whole course of his life, conversed in a familiar manner with his friends and courtiers, and never affected those extraordinary airs of divinity assumed by Alexander and Demetrius.[16] The historian, a contemporary writer, noted for candour and veracity, and withal, the greatest and most penetrating genius, perhaps, of all antiquity; and so free from any tendency to credulity, that he even lies under the contrary imputation, of atheism and profaneness: The persons, from whose authority he related the miracle, of established character for judgement and veracity, as we may well presume; eye-witnesses of the fact, and confirming their testimony, after the Flavian family was despoiled of the empire[17] and could no longer give any reward, as the price of a lie. *Utrumque, qui interfuere, nunc quoque memorant, postquam nullum mendacio pretium.* [Those who were present still tell the tale now, when there is no longer any reward for lying.] To which if we add the public nature of the facts, as related, it will appear, that no evidence can well be supposed stronger for so gross and so palpable a falsehood.

There is also a memorable story related by Cardinal de Retz,[18] which may well deserve our consideration. When that intriguing politician fled into Spain, to avoid the persecution of his enemies, he passed through Saragossa, the capital of Aragon, where he was shewn, in the cathedral, a man, who had served seven years as a doorkeeper, and was well known to every body in town, that had ever paid his devotions at that church. He had been seen, for so long a time, wanting a leg; but recovered that limb by the rubbing of holy oil upon the stump; and the cardinal assures us that he saw him with two legs. This miracle was vouched by all

the canons of the church; and the whole company
in town were appealed to for a confirmation of the
fact; whom the cardinal found, by their zealous
devotion, to be thorough believers of the miracle.
Here the relater was also contemporary to the
supposed prodigy, of an incredulous and libertine
character, as well as of great genius; the miracle of
so *singular* a nature as could scarcely admit of a
counterfeit, and the witnesses very numerous, and
all of them, in a manner, spectators of the fact, to
which they gave their testimony. And what adds
mightily to the force of the evidence, and may
double our surprise on this occasion, is, that the
cardinal himself, who relates the story, seems not
to give any credit to it, and consequently cannot be
suspected of any concurrence in the holy fraud. He
considered justly, that it was not requisite, in order
to reject a fact of this nature, to be able accurately
to disprove the testimony, and to trace its
falsehood, through all the circumstances of knavery
and credulity which produced it. He knew, that, as
this was commonly altogether impossible at any
small distance of time and place; so was it
extremely difficult, even where one was
immediately present, by reason of the bigotry,
ignorance, cunning, and roguery of a great part of
mankind. He therefore concluded, like a just
reasoner, that such an evidence carried falsehood
upon the very face of it, and that a miracle,
supported by any human testimony, was more
properly a subject of derision than of argument.

There surely never was a greater number of
miracles ascribed to one person, than those, which
were lately said to have been wrought in France
upon the tomb of Abbé Paris,[19] the famous

Jansenist, with whose sanctity the people were so long deluded. The curing of the sick, giving hearing to the deaf, and sight to the blind, were every where talked of as the usual effects of that holy sepulchre. But what is more extraordinary; many of the miracles were immediately proved upon the spot, before judges of unquestioned integrity, attested by witnesses of credit and distinction, in a learned age, and on the most eminent theatre that is now in the world. Nor is this all: a relation of them was published and dispersed everywhere; nor were the *Jesuits*, though a learned body, supported by the civil magistrate, and determined enemies to those opinions, in whose favour the miracles were said to have been wrought, ever able distinctly to refute or detect them.[20] Where shall we find such a number of circumstances, agreeing to the corroboration of one fact? And what have we to oppose to such a cloud of witnesses, but the absolute impossibility or miraculous nature of the events, which they relate? And this surely, in the eyes of all reasonable people, will alone be regarded as a sufficient refutation.

This book was writ by Mons. Montgeron, counsellor or judge of the parliament of Paris, a man of figure and character, who was also a martyr to the cause, and is now said to be somewhere in a dungeon on account of his book.

There is another book in three volumes (called *Recueil des Miracles de l'Abbé Paris*) giving an account of many of these miracles, and accompanied with prefatory discourses, which are very well written. There runs, however, through the whole of these a ridiculous comparison between the miracles of our Saviour and those of the Abbé;

wherein it is asserted, that the evidence for the latter is equal to that for the former: As if the testimony of men could ever be put in the balance with that of God himself, who conducted the pen of the inspired writers. If these writers, indeed, were to be considered merely as human testimony, the French author is very moderate in his comparison; since he might, with some appearance of reason, pretend, that the Jansenist miracles much surpass the other in evidence and authority.[21] The following circumstances are drawn from authentic papers, inserted in the above-mentioned book.

Many of the miracles of Abbé Paris were proved immediately by witnesses before the officiality or bishop's court at Paris, under the eye of cardinal Noailles, whose character for integrity and capacity was never contested even by his enemies.

His successor in the archbishopric was an enemy to the Jansenists, and for that reason promoted to the see by the court. Yet 22 rectors or *curés* of Paris, with infinite earnestness, press him to examine those miracles, which they assert to be known to the whole world, and undisputably certain: But he wisely forbore.

The Molinist party had tried to discredit these miracles in one instance, that of Mademoiselle le Franc. But, besides that their proceedings were in many respects the most irregular in the world, particularly in citing only a few of the Jansenist witnesses, whom they tampered with: Besides this, I say, they soon found themselves overwhelmed by a cloud of new witnesses, one hundred and twenty in number, most of them persons of credit and substance in Paris, who gave oath for the miracle. This was accompanied with a solemn and earnest appeal to the parliament. But the parliament were forbidden by authority to meddle in the affair. It was at last observed, that where men are heated by zeal and enthusiasm, there is no degree of human testimony so strong as may not be procured for the greatest absurdity: And those who will be so silly as to examine the affair by that medium, and seek particular flaws in the testimony, are almost sure to be confounded. It must be a miserable imposture, indeed, that does not prevail in that contest.

All who have been in France about that time have heard of the reputation of Mons. Heraut, the *lieutenant de Police*, whose vigilance, penetration, activity, and extensive intelligence have been much talked of. This magistrate, who by the nature of his office is almost absolute, was invested with full powers, on purpose to suppress or discredit these miracles; and he frequently seized immediately, and examined the witnesses and subjects of them: But never could reach any thing satisfactory against them.

In the case of Mademoiselle Thibaut he sent the famous De Sylva to examine her; whose evidence is very curious. The physician declares, that it was impossible she could have been so ill as was proved by witnesses; because it was impossible she could, in so short a time, have recovered so perfectly as he found her. He reasoned, like a man of sense, from natural causes; but the opposite party told him, that the whole was a miracle, and that his evidence was the very best proof of it.

The Molinists were in a sad dilemma. They durst not assert the absolute insufficiency of human evidence, to prove a miracle. They were obliged to say, that these miracles were wrought by witchcraft and the devil. But they were told, that this was the resource of the Jews of old.

No Jansenist was ever embarrassed to account for the cessation of the miracles, when the church-yard was shut up by the king's edict. It was the touch of the tomb, which produced these extraordinary effects; and when no one could approach the tomb, no effects could be expected. God, indeed, could have thrown down the walls in a moment; but he is master of his own graces and works, and it belongs not to us to account for them. He did not throw down the walls of every city like those of Jericho, on the sounding of the rams horns, nor break up the prison of every apostle, like that of St. Paul.

No less a man, than the Duc de Chatillon, a duke and peer of France, of the highest rank and family, gives evidence of a miraculous cure, performed upon a servant of his, who had lived several years in his house with a visible and palpable infirmity.

I shall conclude with observing, that no clergy are more celebrated for strictness of life and manners than the secular clergy of France, particularly the rectors or curés of Paris, who bear testimony to these impostures.

The learning, genius, and probity of the gentlemen, and the austerity of the nuns of Port-Royal, have been much celebrated all over Europe. Yet they all give evidence for a miracle, wrought on the niece of the famous Pascal, whose sanctity of life, as well as extraordinary capacity, is well known. The famous Racine gives an account of this miracle in his famous history of Port-Royal,

and fortifies it with all the proofs, which a
multitude of nuns, priests, physicians, and men of
the world, all of them of undoubted credit, could
bestow upon it. Several men of letters, particularly
the bishop of Tournay, thought this miracle so
certain, as to employ it in the refutation of atheists
and freethinkers. The queen-regent of France, who
was extremely prejudiced against the Port-Royal,
sent her own physician to examine the miracle,
who returned an absolute convert. In short, the
supernatural cure was so uncontestable, that it
saved, for a time, that famous monastery from the
ruin with which it was threatened by the Jesuits.
Had it been a cheat, it had certainly been detected
by such sagacious and powerful antagonists, and
must have hastened the ruin of the contrivers. Our
divines, who can build up a formidable castle from
such despicable materials; what a prodigious fabric
could they have reared from these and many other
circumstances, which I have not mentioned! How
often would the great names of Pascal, Racine,
Arnaud, Nicole, have resounded in our ears? But if
they be wise, they had better adopt the miracle, as
being more worth, a thousand times, than all the
rest of their collection. Besides, it may serve very
much to their purpose. For that miracle was really
performed by the touch of an authentic holy prickle
of the holy thorn, which composed the holy crown,
which, &c.

    Is the consequence just, because some human
testimony has the utmost force and authority in
some cases, when it relates the battle of Philippi or
Pharsalia for instance;[22] that therefore all kinds of
testimony must, in all cases, have equal force and
authority? Suppose that the Caesarean and

Pompeian factions had, each of them, claimed the victory in these battles, and that the historians of each party had uniformly ascribed the advantage to their own side; how could mankind, at this distance, have been able to determine between them? The contrariety is equally strong between the miracles related by Herodotus or Plutarch, and those delivered by Mariana, Bede, or any monkish historian.[23]

The wise lend a very academic faith to every report which favours the passion of the reporter; whether it magnifies his country, his family, or himself, or in any other way strikes in with his natural inclinations and propensities. But what greater temptation than to appear a missionary, a prophet, an ambassador from heaven? Who would not encounter many dangers and difficulties, in order to attain so sublime a character? Or if, by the help of vanity and a heated imagination, a man has first made a convert of himself, and entered seriously into the delusion; who ever scruples to make use of pious frauds, in support of so holy and meritorious a cause?

The smallest spark may here kindle into the greatest flame; because the materials are always prepared for it. The *avidum genus auricularum,*[24] the gazing populace, receive greedily, without examination, whatever soothes superstition, and promotes wonder.

How many stories of this nature have, in all ages, been detected and exploded in their infancy? How many more have been celebrated for a time, and have afterwards sunk into neglect and oblivion? Where such reports, therefore, fly about, the solution of the phenomenon is obvious; and we judge in conformity to regular experience and observation, when we account for it by the known and natural principles of credulity and delusion. And shall we, rather than have a recourse to so natural a solution, allow of a miraculous violation of the most established laws of nature?

I need not mention the difficulty of detecting a falsehood in any private or even public history, at the place, where it is said to happen; much more when the scene is removed to ever so small a distance. Even a court of judicature, with all the authority, accuracy, and judgement, which they can employ, find themselves often at a loss to distinguish between truth and falsehood in the most recent actions. But the matter never comes to any issue, if trusted to the common method of altercation and debate and flying rumours; especially when men's passions have taken part on either side.

In the infancy of new religions, the wise and learned commonly esteem the matter too inconsiderable to deserve their attention or regard. And when afterwards they would willingly detect the cheat, in order to undeceive the deluded multitude, the season is now past, and the records and witnesses, which might clear up the matter, have perished beyond recovery.

No means of detection remain, but those which must be drawn from the very testimony itself of the reporters: and these, though always sufficient with the judicious and knowing, are commonly too fine to fall under the comprehension of the vulgar.

Upon the whole, then, it appears, that no testimony for any kind of miracle has ever amounted to a probability, much less to a proof;

and that, even supposing it amounted to a proof, it would be opposed by another proof; derived from the very nature of the fact, which it would endeavour to establish. It is experience only, which gives authority to human testimony; and it is the same experience, which assures us of the laws of nature. When, therefore, these two kinds of experience are contrary, we have nothing to do but subtract the one from the other, and embrace an opinion, either on one side or the other, with that assurance which arises from the remainder. But according to the principle here explained, this substraction, with regard to all popular religions, amounts to an entire annihilation; and therefore we may establish it as a maxim, that no human testimony can have such force as to prove a miracle, and make it a just foundation for any such system of religion.

I beg the limitations here made may be remarked, when I say, that a miracle can never be proved, so as to be the foundation of a system of religion. For I own, that otherwise, there may possibly be miracles, or violations of the usual course of nature, of such a kind as to admit of proof from human testimony; though, perhaps, it wil be impossible to find any such in all the records of history. Thus, suppose, all authors, in all languages, agree, that, from the first of January 1600, there was a total darkness over the whole earth for eight days: suppose that the tradition of this extraordinary event is still strong and lively among the people: that all travellers, who return from foreign countries, bring us accounts of the same tradition, without the least variation or contradiction: it is evident, that our present philosophers, instead of doubting the fact, ought to receive it as certain, and ought to search for the causes whence it might be derived. The decay, corruption, and dissolution of nature, is an event rendered probable by so many analogies, that any phenomenon, which seems to have a tendency towards that catastrophe, comes within the reach of human testimony, if that testimony be very extensive and uniform.

But suppose, that all the historians who treat of England, should agree, that, on the first of January 1600, Queen Elizabeth died; that both before and after her death she was seen by her physicians and the whole court, as is usual with persons of her rank; that her successor was acknowledged and proclaimed by the parliament; and that, after being interred a month, she again appeared, resumed the throne, and governed England for three years: I must confess that I should be surprised at the concurrence of so many odd circumstances, but should not have the least inclination to believe so miraculous an event. I should not doubt of her pretended death, and of those other public circumstances that followed it: I should only assert it to have been pretended, and that it neither was, nor possibly could be real. You would in vain object to me the difficulty, and almost impossibility of deceiving the world in an affair of such consequence; the wisdom and solid judgement of that renowned queen; with the little or no advantage which she could reap from so poor an artifice: All this might astonish me; but I would still reply, that the knavery and folly of men are such common phenomena, that I should rather believe the most extraordinary events to arise from their concurrence, than admit of so signal a violation of the laws of nature.

But should this miracle be ascribed to any new system of religion; men, in all ages, have been so much imposed on by ridiculous stories of that kind, that this very circumstance would be a full proof of a cheat, and sufficient, with all men of sense, not only to make them reject the fact, but even reject it without farther examination. Though the Being to whom the miracle is ascribed, be, in this case, Almighty, it does not, upon that account, become a whit more probable; since it is impossible for us to know the attributes or actions of such a Being, otherwise than from the experience which we have of his productions, in the usual course of nature. This still reduces us to past observation, and obliges us to compare the instances of the violation of truth in the testimony of men, with those of the violation of the laws of nature by miracles, in order to judge which of them is most likely and probable. As the violations of truth are more common in the testimony concerning religious miracles, than in that concerning any other matter of fact; this must diminish very much the authority of the former testimony, and make us form a general resolution, never to lend any attention to it, with whatever specious pretence it may be covered.

Lord Bacon seems to have embraced the same principles of reasonings.[25] 'We ought,' says he, 'to make a collection or particular history of all monsters and prodigious births or productions, and in a word of every thing new, rare, and extraordinary in nature. But this must be done with the most severe scrutiny, lest we depart from truth. Above all, every relation must be considered as suspicious, which depends in any degree upon religion, as the prodigies of Livy: And no less so, every thing that is to be found in the writers of natural magic or alchimy, or such authors, who seem, all of them, to have an unconquerable appetite for falsehood and fable.'

I am the better pleased with the method of reasoning here delivered, as I think it may serve to confound those dangerous friends or disguised enemies to the *Christian Religion*, who have undertaken to defend it by the principles of human reason. Our most holy religion is founded on *Faith*, not on reason; and it is a sure method of exposing it to put it to such a trial as it is, by no means, fitted to endure. To make this more evident, let us examine those miracles, related in scripture; and not to lose ourselves in too wide a field, let us confine ourselves to such as we find in the *Pentateuch*,[26] which we shall examine, according to the principles of these pretended Christians, not as the word or testimony of God himself, but as the production of a mere human writer and historian. Here then we are first to consider a book, presented to us by a barbarous and ignorant people, written in an age when they were still more barbarous, and in all probability long after the facts which it relates, corroborated by no concurring testimony, and resembling those fabulous accounts, which every nation gives of its origin. Upon reading this book, we find it full of prodigies and miracles. It gives an account of a state of the world and of human nature entirely different from the present: Of our fall from that state: Of the age of man, extended to near a thousand years: Of the destruction of the world by a deluge: Of the arbitrary choice of one people, as the favourites of heaven; and that people the countrymen of the author: Of their deliverance from bondage by prodigies the most astonishing imaginable: I desire any one to lay his hand upon his heart, and after a serious consideration declare, whether he thinks that the falsehood of such a book, supported by such a testimony, would be more extraordinary and miraculous than all the miracles it relates; which is, however, necessary to make it be received, according to the measures of probability above established.

What we have said of miracles may be applied, without any variation, to prophecies; and indeed, all prophecies are real miracles, and as such only, can be admitted as proofs of any revelation. If it did not exceed the capacity of human nature to foretell future events, it would be absurd to employ any prophecy as an argument for a divine mission or authority from heaven. So that, upon the whole, we may conclude, that the *Christian Religion* not only was at first attended with miracles, but even at this day cannot be believed by any reasonable person without one. Mere reason is insufficient to convince us of its veracity: And whoever is moved by *Faith* to assent to it, is conscious of a continued miracle in his own person, which subverts all the principles of his understanding, and gives him a determination to believe what is most contrary to custom and experience.[27]

Notes

1. John Tillotson (1630–94) was an influential Presbyterian clergyman who in 1662 submitted to the Act of Uniformity. In 1691 he was appointed Archbishop of Canterbury. Reference works tell us, tactfully, that "in later years his sermons emphasized the practical . . . rather than the theological aspects of Christianity".

Certainly the fact that he appears to have believed that the doctrine of the Real Presence, as construed by Roman Catholics, actually contradicts sensory experience, suggests a remarkable lack of theological sophistication. For the peculiarly Roman Catholic doctrine of Transubstantiation, explaining how it is supposed to be possible to be really present though wholly unobservable, is a doctrine maintaining that, in a properly conducted Mass, the substance of the bread and the substance of the wine are transformed into the substance of the body and the substance of the blood of the Christ, *all the sensory appearances remaining the same.*

2. 'Moral evidence' here means evidence from and about matters of fact. The contrast is with matters which can be demonstrated as deducible from logically necessary truths. It is the same use of the word 'moral' as in the fossil phrase 'moral certainty'.

3. Here and subsequently Hume should have written not 'experiments' but 'experiences'.

4. Cato the Younger (95–46 B.C.), a Roman politician and

56

moralist, described as "a philosophical patriot" because of his adhesion to the Stoic philosophy.

5. The reference here is to John Locke *An Essay Concerning Human Understanding*, III (vi) 13 and IV (xvi) 5–6. The "first relations" are the first stories related.

6. In Hume's original, this paragraph was a footnote.

7. This paragraph was originally printed as a footnote.

8. An enthusiast in the eighteenth century was a fanatic. So the epigraphic tributes in English churches to divines who were "religious but without enthusiasm" lacked for contemporaries the piquant flavour which they have for us today!

9. Tully was Marcus Tullius Cicero (106–43 B.C.), a Roman politician and orator. His various, wholly derivative philosophical work, mainly written in the last few months before his political murder, were extremely influential in Hume's day; partly because the sources from which they were derived have been largely lost. Demosthenes (384–322 B.C.) was an Athenian politician and orator. A Capuchin is a Friar of one branch of the order of St. Francis.

10. Lucian, in the second century A.D., was a Greek satirical writer. His *Alexander, or the False Prophet* was an account of the faking of a manifestation of Asclepius, (Aesculapius) a god of healing, in the form of a serpent with a human head. Paphlagonia was a territory in the north of what is now Asiatic Turkey.

11. Marcus Aurelius (121–80 A.D.) was at this time the Roman Emperor, and thus the supreme ruler over Paphlagonia. He was an adherent of the Stoic philosophy, and author of the classic *Meditations*.

12. 'Mahomet' was the older spelling of Mohammed (c.570–632 A.D.), the Prophet of Islam.

13. Titus Livius (59 B.C.–17 A.D.) was a Roman historian of Rome, more usually referred to as Livy. Plutarch (c.46–c.120 A.D.) was a Greek writer of biographies—the 'parallel lives'. Hume refers to his *Life of Cato* in a note to the mention in Part I, above. Tacitus (c.57 A.D.–c.120 A.D.) was a notably sceptical and astringent Roman historian of Imperial Rome.

14. Vespasian (9–79 A.D.) was a tough and successful soldier who became a Roman Emperor. Fully to appreciate this story you need to recognize that Vespasian and his soldiers,

whether rightly or wrongly, amply had the same contempt for Egyptians as was common in the British Eighth Army during World War II.

15. Hume here refers us to Tacitus *Histories* V 8, and this reference has been reprinted in every successive edition of the *First Inquiry* from 1777 until Peter Nidditch's 1975 revision of L. A. Selby-Bigge's long standard Clarendon Press version. It would seem that—notwithstanding all the controversy which there has been about this Section X 'Of Miracles'—no one ever looked the passage up in Tacitus until I did this in preparing my *Hume's Philosophy of Belief* (London: Routledge and Kegan Paul, 1961). I then discovered that 'V 8' should have been 'IV 81'. Several morals may be drawn from this remarkable fact.

Hume also notes that the inferior authority Suetonius (c.69–c.140 A.D.) gives a similar account in his life of Vespasian.

16. Alexander the Great (356–323 B.C.) and Demetrius I of Macedonia (336–283 B.C.).

17. The Flavian Emperors were Vespasian and his sons Titus (c.40–81 A.D.) and Domitian (51–96 A.D.)

18. Cardinal de Retz (1614–79) was an Archbishop of Paris, author of *Mémoires*.

19. François de Paris (1690–1727) was a follower of Cornelius Jansen (1585–1638), a Bishop of Ypres in Flanders. Jansenism was a doctrine of moral austerity and of the dependence of all virtue on divine grace, a doctrine expounded most notably in Jansen's 1640 *Augustinus*. It was adopted by the Cistercian Convent of Port-Royal, with which the mathematician and philosopher Blaise Pascal (1623–62) and other leading French intellectuals were closely associated. Among these Arnauld and Nicole produced in 1662 *L'Art du Penser*, a very influential work usually known as the *Port-Royal Logic*.

As Hume proceeds to make clear, the question of the genuineness of the miracles supposedly occurring "upon the tomb of Abbé Paris" was crucial for both the Jansenists and their Jesuit opponents. For they were agreed that the ocurrence of any genuine miracles must constitute decisive Divine endorsement for the doctrinal claims of the party thus favoured.

20. At this point in Hume's original came the reference to

a gleeful footnote, 12 paragraphs long, giving more details of the miracles allegedly wrought on and around the tomb of the Abbé Paris. The footnote, commencing "This book was writ by Mons. Montgeron", is here incorporated into the text.

21. Many readers, including too many of those paid to know better, have, both here and elsewhere, failed to recognize Hume's irony. It may, therefore, be necessary to indicate that, of course, he himself regarded this comparison not as ridiculous but rather as totally to the point and absolutely devastating.

22. Philippi was a city in Macedonia where in 42 B.C. the army of Octavian, the future first Roman Emperor Augustus, and Mark Antony, defeated the republican army: see, for instance, Shakespeare's *Julius Caesar*. Pharsalia was a city in Thessaly, a part of what is now Northern Greece, near where in 48 B.C. Caesar's army defeated that of Pompey.

23. Herodotus of Halicarnassus in Asia Minor was a Greek historian working in the fifth century B.C. Generally allowed to be 'the father of history' Herodotus normally dissociates himself from whatever tales of the seemingly miraculous he feels bound to record. Juan Mariana (1536–1623 A.D.) was a Spanish Jesuit who wrote Spanish history. St. Bede (c.673–735 A.D.) is often called, perhaps too flatteringly, 'the father of Engish history.'

24. This phrase ['race eager for hearsay'] is taken from the secularizing Roman poet Lucretius *(de Rerum Natura* [On the Nature of Things] IV 594).

25. Francis Bacon (1561–1626) under James I, and until his disgrace in an earlier Water Gate affair, was Lord Chancellor of England. Bacon is usually rated the first in the long line of British empiricist philosophers. The passage quoted is Aphorism 29 of Book II of his *Novum Organum*, a work in which he tried to improve upon previous conceptions of scientific method.

26. 'Pentateuch' is a term for the first five books of the *Old Testament* (Genesis, Exodus, Leviticus, Numbers, and Deuteronomy.)

27. This final paragraph has been seen as more scandalous than any other passage in all Hume's writings. Fully to understand and to savour it we need to know what was, in his day, the regular teaching of all the Reformed Churches. Faith,

it was held, or even a correct reading of the Scriptures, is impossible save to those vouch-safed Divine Grace; a Grace miraculously, and it would seem arbitrarily, conferred upon all but only the Elect.